Alphabet Books

Animal Babies ABC

An Alphabet Book of Animal Offspring

by Barbara Knox

Consultant:
Brandie Smith
Assistant Director, Conservation and Science
American Zoo and Aquarium Association

Capstone
press
Mankato, Minnesota

A is for alligator.

Alligator babies hatch from eggs. The babies croak
to let the mother know that they hatched.

B is for bear.

Bear cubs do not have teeth when they are born. Cubs drink milk from their mothers.

C is for cat.

Cats have litters of kittens. Some
kittens run and play outside.

Aa Bb Cc Dd Ee Ff Gg Hh Ii Jj Kk Ll Mm Nn Oo Pp Qq Rr Ss Tt Uu Vv Ww Xx Yy Zz

D is for dog.

Dogs and puppies cannot
sweat. They pant to keep cool.

E is for elephant.

A female elephant has one calf at a time. She teaches her calf how to use its trunk to drink and find food.

F is for frog.

Female frogs lay many eggs. The eggs hatch into tadpoles. Tadpoles look like small fish.

G is for giraffe.

Giraffe cows give birth
standing up. Baby giraffes
tumble down to the ground.
The fall does not hurt them.

H is for horse.

A newborn foal stands up soon after it is born. It can run after a few hours.

I is for ibex.

Ibex babies are called kids.
Kids follow their mothers
up steep cliffs.

J is for jaguar.

Jaguar cubs are good climbers and swimmers. They have sharp claws.

K is for koala.

A koala lives in its mother's pouch for the first
part of its life. It climbs out when it grows too big
for the pouch.

Aa Bb Cc Dd Ee Ff Gg Hh Ii Jj **Kk** Ll Mm Nn Oo Pp Qq Rr Ss Tt Uu Vv Ww Xx Yy Zz

L is for llama.

Female llamas give birth to one baby at a time. The baby is called a cria.

M is for moose.

Moose calves hear well. Their large ears move to hear different sounds.

N is for nightingale.

Nightingale chicks stay safe
in a nest. They wait for their
mother to bring bugs for
them to eat.

O is for otter.

At first, otter pups are small and helpless. They stay with their mother for about one year.

P is for penguin.

Penguin chicks rest atop a
parent's claws. From there,
the chicks stay safe and snug.

Q is for quail.

Quail chicks take about 18 days to hatch. A few hours after they hatch, quail chicks can walk, eat, and drink.

R is for raccoon.

Raccoon kits spend most of
their time climbing trees.
They eat animals and plants.

19

Aa Bb Cc Dd Ee Ff Gg Hh Ii Jj Kk Ll Mm
Nn Oo Pp Qq Rr **Ss** Tt Uu Vv Ww Xx Yy Zz

S is for sheep.

Baby sheep are called
lambs. Lambs and sheep
are very good jumpers.

20

T is for tiger.

Tiger cubs drink milk from their mother. They stay with their mother for about two years.

21

U is for porcupine.

Porcupines have many soft quills
when they are born. The quills
harden and become sharp after
a few hours.

V is for viper.

Eyelash viper snakes give birth to live young.

The young snakes eat lizards, frogs, and birds.

W is for walrus.

Walrus calves have whiskers. The whiskers help them find food.

Aa Bb Cc Dd Ee Ff Gg Hh Ii Jj Kk Ll Mm Nn Oo Pp Qq Rr Ss Tt Uu Vv Ww Xx Yy Zz

X is for fox.

Foxes look like small dogs. Fox kits leave
their parents after a few months.

Y is for yak.

Yak calves live with their mothers in a herd.

They run, leap, and climb.

Z is for zebra.

Zebra foals run soon after they are born. Their mothers stay close by and watch over them.

Animal Offspring Facts

Alligator
- lays 25 to 60 eggs in a nest
- lives in swamps

Bear
- female is a sow; male is a boar
- cubs are born in a den

Cat
- born in litters of three to six kittens
- female is a queen; male is a tom

Dog
- drinks milk from its mother
- born with eyes closed

Elephant
- female is a cow; male is a bull
- one calf is born at a time

Frog
- born in water, but live on land
- group of frogs is called an army

Giraffe
- has short horns
- uses long neck to reach high trees

Horse
- male foal is a colt
- female foal is a filly

Ibex
- lives in rocky areas in Africa and Europe
- one to two kids born at a time

Jaguar
- cubs are born in a den
- born with eyes closed

Koala
- newborns are the size of jellybeans
- young are called joeys

Llama
- has wooly fur
- related to camels

Moose
- largest member of the deer family
- name means "eater of twigs"

Nightingale
- is a songbird
- lays green eggs

Otter

- swims using webbed toes
- pups stay with mothers for one year

Penguin

- has wings but cannot fly
- parents take turns hatching eggs

Quail

- adult hen lays 300 eggs yearly
- eats insects and vegetation

Raccoon

- kits growl, hiss, and snort
- most active at night

Sheep

- has a wooly coat
- two to three lambs born at a time

Tiger

- largest member of the cat family
- male cubs grow faster than female cubs

Porcupine

- is a rodent
- has one to two young at a time

Viper

- has live young; many snakes lay eggs
- can go one year without eating

Walrus

- lives in herds
- calves grow tusks

Fox

- females have litters of three to five kits
- kits are born with their eyes closed

Yak

- both males and females have horns
- lives in Tibetan mountains

Zebra

- one foal born at a time
- foals drink milk for one year

Words to Know

hatch (HACH)—to break out of an egg; some animals sit on their eggs to keep them warm.

herd (HURD)—a large group of animals that live together; animals in herds often protect each other.

litter (LIT-ur)—a group of animals born at the same time to one mother

nest (NEST)—a place built by birds or other animals to lay their eggs; birds use mud, sticks, and other materials to build nests.

Read More

Simon, Seymour. *Baby Animals.* SeeMore Readers. New York: SeaStar Books, 2002.

Singer, Marilyn. *Tough Beginnings: How Baby Animals Survive.* New York: Henry Holt, 2001.

Wallace, Karen. *Wild Baby Animals.* Eyewitness Readers. New York: DK Publishing, 2000.

Wilson, Sarah. *A Nap in a Lap.* New York: Henry Holt, 2003.

Internet Sites

Track down many sites about baby animals. Visit the FACT HOUND at
http://www.facthound.com

IT IS EASY! IT IS FUN!

1) Go to *http://www.facthound.com*
2) Type in: 0736816801
3) Click on "FETCH IT" and FACT HOUND will find several links hand-picked by our editors.

Relax and let our pal FACT HOUND do the research for you!

Index

32

A+ Books are published by Capstone Press
P.O. Box 669, 151 Good Counsel Drive, Mankato, Minnesota 56002
http://www.capstone-press.com

1 2 3 4 5 6 08 07 06 05 04 03

Library of Congress Cataloging-in-Publication Data
Knox, Barbara
Animal babies ABC: an alphabet book of animal offspring/by Barbara Knox.
p. cm.—(Alphabet books)
Summary: Introduces baby animals through photographs and text that describe one animal for each letter of the alphabet.
Includes bibliographical references (p. 31) and index.
ISBN 0-7368-1680-1 (hardcover)
1. Animals—Infancy—Juvenile literature. 2. English language—Alphabet—Juvenile literature. [1. Animals—Infancy. 2. Alphabet.] I. Title. II. Series: Alphabet books (Mankato, Minn.)
QL763 .K66 2003
591.3'9—dc21   2002015065

Credits
Sarah L. Schuette, editor; Heather Kindseth, designer; Patrick D. Dentinger, illustrator; Juliette Peters, cover production; Deirdre Barton, photo researcher
Photo Credits
Alan Blank/Bruce Coleman, Inc., 18
Buddy Mays/Travel Stock Photography, 20
Corbis, front cover, 5, 9, 24, 30; Darrell Gulin, 2; John W. Herbst, 3; Elio Ciol, 6; Michael & Patricia Fogden, 7, 23; AFP, 8; Steve Kaufman, 10; D. Robert & Lorri Franz, 11; Theo Allofs, 12; Wolfgang Kaehler, 13; Randy M. Ury, 14; Lynda Richardson, 15; Tim Davis, 17; W. Perry Conway, 19; Terry Whittaker, 21; Nigel J. Dennis, 25; Jonathan Blair, 26; Joe McDonald, 27
Creatas, 22
Digital Vision, 4
PhotoDisc, Inc., back cover
Sea World San Diego, 16

Note to Parents, Teachers, and Librarians
Animal Babies ABC uses color photographs and a nonfiction format to introduce children to the various animals and their young while building mastery of the alphabet. It is designed to be read aloud to a pre-reader or to be read independently by an early reader. The images help early readers and listeners understand the text and concepts discussed. The book encourages further learning by including the following sections: Animal Offspring Facts, Words to Know, Read More, Internet Sites, and Index. Early readers may need assistance using these features.